THE JOURNEY TO MARS

A Young Minds Guide To The Solar System,
Space Exploration and How To Get To Mars!

Jordan Moore

ISBN: 979-8-88768-019-4

CONTENTS

INTRODUCTION

PSSCCHT! *Ground control to the future-bestest-amazingest-incrediblest-astronaut-ever. Your mission has arrived! You will be one of the first people to travel to Mars and the first person to ever* **live** *there.*

But how? Well, this book is here to help guide you along the long and complicated journey toward becoming the most important astronaut of all time. What you read on these pages will be a frankly stupendous amount of information about the biggest topic there is: *space*.

Douglas Adams was right when he once wrote:

"Space is big. Really big. You just won't believe how vastly, hugely, mind-bogglingly big it is."

It quite simply is a huge thing. Human beings have explored so much of Earth. We've put submarines at the bottom of the ocean, jumbo jets above the clouds, and charted every piece of land on the planet. Now we need to discover more about space and find out what secrets lay in wait for us.

Throughout this book, you will discover how to become an astronaut, what happens to us in space, what evidence we have of aliens, and much more. You'll go through your journey step by step until you reach Mars in Chapter Ten.

Be prepared for the massive amount of fantastical, excellent knowledge that you're about to learn. You're going to become a real clever-clogs. Whenever there's a debate about space, astronauts, and Mars to be had, you'd better be the first person who is asked for their opinion.

This book may be the first step for you as you dedicate your life to becoming a world-famous explorer and astronaut. Or it may just be an interesting read, which is also fine! Either way, enjoy learning about the journey to Mars and the most epic exploration of space in all human history.

P.S. There's a glossary at the back of the book to help you with some space terms. Use this glossary if there's a word you don't understand.

WHAT IS THE
SOLAR SYSTEM?

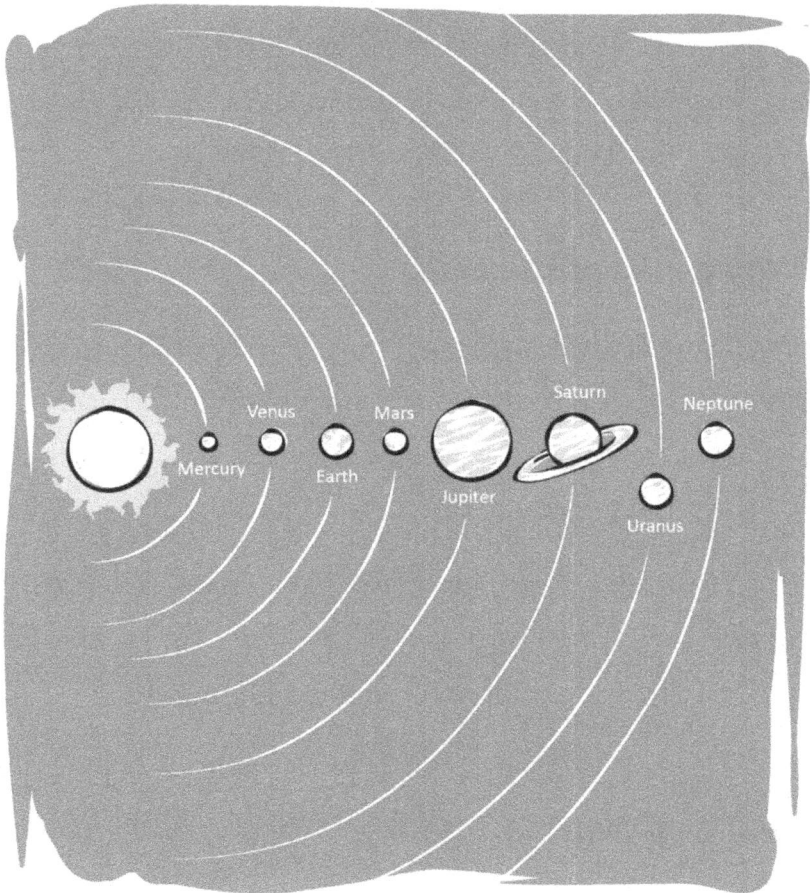

So, you're going to Mars! Fantastic! Everyone on Earth is confident that you're the best person for the job and won't *completely* mess it up. Our first step is all about education. How are you meant to find your way to Mars if you don't know the first thing about it?

In this first chapter, you'll learn a bit about the Solar System, and the galaxy that we live in and you will be exploring. Pay close attention to this! You may well need to know all this smart stuff when you're trying to get to Mars.

1. Who's part of the club?

You are in the Solar System right now. This is the name given to an area that we are part of and is made up of the Sun (called Sol), eight planets, many moons, asteroids, comets, and other objects.

There are many hundreds of thousands of millions of galaxies out there! We think that there may in fact be an *infinite* number of galaxies (which means that there's no end to the number of galaxies that there are). But none are the same as ours.

Our Sun is a star. It is the center of our system and all the other planets revolve around it, receiving heat and light from it. Those planets are - Mercury, Venus, Earth, Mars, Jupiter, Saturn, Uranus, and Neptune. But the Sun is just one of several thousands of stars that are part of the Milky Way galaxy.

A great way to remember the planets in the Solar System is using the pneumonic: "My Very Educated Mother Just Served Us Noodles"!

2. Earth is unique

The planets in the Solar System are all very different from one another, though Earth remains a completely unique planet for one very specific reason: We are living on it.

As far as we know at this time, no other planet in our galaxy has anything living on it. There's some evidence that Mars might be able to sustain life, but nothing has been proven for sure on that front yet.

But why Earth? Why this place?

There are several reasons for this, but the most important one is that the Earth is *exactly* the right distance from the Sun. The Earth is just close enough to the Sun so that the planet is kept at an average of 59°F, with some hotter bits and some colder bits. This means that life can grow and survive easier than on a planet such as Mars, which sits at -85°F!

Another *hugely* crucial reason is that Earth constantly has water on it. As far as we know, all life needs water, and no other planet in the galaxy has it! Because of these main features, Earth is a unique planet that has actual things living on it.

3. Solar system? More like So-old-ar system!

It can become bafflingly complicated when we think about just how old space and the universe are. How can we tell? Well, through incredibly complicated scientific workings out from NASA!

NASA is quite sure that the Solar System formed about 4.5 billion years ago. There was a large cloud of gas and dust that suddenly collapsed. This probably happened because a star exploded nearby, and it caused the material to spin and swirl. As this occurred, the cloud's gravity dragged more and more material toward its center and clumps were formed. These clumps became the parts of the Solar System we recognize today, such as the Sun and planets!

This process took a very long time, it wasn't an immediate process. But we believe that this is what caused the Solar System to happen at all! It can be confusing, but NASA scientists are quite sure that this is accurate, and we can even find little 4.5-billion-year-old 'clumps' flying around the Solar System today!

4. Gas mass

Earth is essentially a large rock, made up of several layers and materials. It's pretty solid, and thousands of degrees hot at its center. But not every planet is like this; in fact, half of the planets in the Solar System aren't made of dense rock at all but are largely made from gases.

The 'outer planets' (the furthest from the Sun) - Jupiter, Saturn, Uranus, and Neptune - are all known as 'gas planets' because they're mainly made from hydrogen and helium. At their center, they have a solid core, but you'd struggle to walk on them! You'd have to somehow battle through swirling layers of liquids and gasses, none of which is breathable, even before you got anywhere near the inhospitable core.

The gas planets often have many moons orbiting them, and some (such as Jupiter and Saturn) have colossal rings around them made of dust and debris.

Traveling to any of these planets poses unique challenges, such as where do you land the spacecraft.

5. In constant motion

This fact can become a little bit baffling, so read it slowly and try not to think *too hard* about it.

It takes the Earth 24 hours to complete one full rotation. This is why there are 24 hours per day. This means that the Earth has to spin at a speed of 1,037 miles per hour. If a car could go that fast, it could drive across the United States of America in just over two-and-a-half hours. That's pretty fast!

But that's not all. The Earth is also spinning around the Sun, as is every planet. It takes the Earth 365.25 days to complete its journey, which is why every year is 365 days (apart from leap years, which are 366). For the Earth to do *this*, it travels at a speed of about 67,000 miles per hour!

And somewhat more shocking than this is that the whole Solar System is also hurtling through space, taking us with it. The reason is that our entire system is also orbiting the center of the Milky Way. The Solar System, which means the Sun, the planets, the moons, the dust, the comets, meteorites, and everything, is zooming by at a speed of 448,000 miles per hour!

It's mind-boggling stuff. What's even more mind-boggling is that all this happens without even messing up your hair…

6. The gravity of the situation

In the whirling chaos of the Universe, with its billions of years of history and constant movement, one question is on everyone's minds at a certain age:

Why am I not flying through space right now? What keeps me on Earth?

That's a fantastic question if you thought of it - and if you didn't think of it, then thank God someone did. The answer is quite simply one word: gravity.

Gravity is a force that pulls things toward the center of a big object. Think about how everything explained above is spinning (or orbiting) something else. Earth spins around the Sun, and the Sun spins around the center of the galaxy. This is all happening because of gravity.

We aren't 100% sure exactly *why* gravity works yet, but we do know *how* it works. When a large object is spinning very fast, it pulls other objects toward it, into its pull. The weight of the object will change how strongly it's pulled toward the bigger one.

So, as Earth is spinning around and around, it creates a gravitational force. This force keeps you glued to the planet and draws things to the center of the planet. When you drop something, the reason it falls *down* and not *up* is that gravity is pulling it toward the center of the Earth. Gravity also affects everything at the same rate; you don't get more gravity if you're heavier!

Bit confusing, eh? Well, try this experiment out somewhere outdoors:

1) Get two plastic bottles (they must be the same size and type of bottle).
2) Half-fill one with water, and leave the other empty.

You'll probably think that if you were to drop these bottles, the heavier one (the half-filled one) should fall faster, right? Try this:

1) Stand on something, to gain a bit of height, and drop both bottles at the same time from the same height.

2) Both bottles should hit the ground at the same time, every time.

This is because it doesn't seem to matter how heavy you are, gravity works in the same way. It only matters how *big* something is.

7. Tighten your belt

You might have heard of an asteroid before in a movie or a book. You may have even held one before, you just didn't know it....

Asteroids are rocky objects that orbit the Sun, much like planets do, though they're far smaller. Asteroids can be found all over the Solar System. Some of them follow Earth, trapped in its gravity. They are left over from the creation of the Solar System 4.6 billion years ago; they're basically scrap material that the star system didn't use.

Asteroids can cause problems for space travel, so you'll have to keep a close eye out for them! Just make sure you avoid the asteroid belt that's between Jupiter and Mars. It's a colossal ring of solid asteroids and small planets, and you'll want to not go anywhere near it if you fancy flying away again.

Sometimes a small part of an asteroid called a meteorite flies into Earth's atmosphere and lands on our surface. It's totally harmless provided it doesn't hit something. We believe that an asteroid hit planet Earth about 60 million years ago, killing the dinosaurs and 90% of life on Earth. So yeah, try to stay away from them.

8. Going dark

Sometimes we experience strange events on Earth called *eclipses*. Experiencing an eclipse will bring darkness to an area of Earth in the middle of the day. You could be in perfect sunlight one minute, then in the night light the next!

This all happens when the Sun and Moon line up. The Moon blocks the sunlight from reaching the Earth, plunging the affected area into darkness! This happens regularly, as the Moon spins around the Earth and the Earth spins around the Sun, about four to seven times a year!

Though it happens quite regularly, you probably won't see one most years. The affected areas are at very specific points across the world, so having time to experience one is rare and should be savored.

If you hear that a solar eclipse will happen in your part of the world, then you should try to go outside and experience it for yourself. You should hopefully see a dark circle in the sky with a halo of light around it, plunging you into nighttime. Make sure you don't stare straight at it, however, as it can damage your eyes!

9. Like, comet, and subscribe

There's another, more visible, thing that flies through space other than an asteroid, and that is a comet. Comets are big, icy space rocks that are zooming about through space.

Comets are made up of rock, ice, and dust. They have a tail that glows and is even visible when the comet draws close to a star. These aren't small tails either, they can be millions of kilometers long!

Comets are, like all objects, in an orbit around the Sun. They all have different paths and different orbits. This means that some comets can be seen quite often whereas others such as Halley's Comet are less commonly spotted. Halley's Comet was first spotted in 239 BCE, and flies past the Earth every 75–79 years! Scientists and star-watchers are eagerly looking forward to the 2060s when the comet is likely to next pass us by.

Comets are amazing things and the study of them could provide important answers about the origins of the Universe. In 2004, a spacecraft landed on a comet and helped us to study some strange objects.

10. Gargantuan geography

Obviously, Earth is home to some amazing geography. We have colossal mountain ranges, vast oceans, and fearsome storms that tear apart our landscapes. It's an awesome planet when you come to think of it.

However, the other planets in the Solar System seem able to beat us on most things, apart from our sea.

For instance, Mars is home to the largest mountain in the Solar System, called Olympus Mons. It has a height of about 16 miles! That makes it three times as tall as the famous Mount Everest here on Earth.

Though we have scary tsunamis, typhoons, and hurricanes, Jupiter has a storm that makes our extreme weather look a bit pathetic. Currently, a great storm called the Great Red Spot rages in Jupiter - and has been doing so for more than 300 years! The storm is so large that you could fit three Earths inside of it.

Saturn possesses several moons, and one of them, Enceladus, is home to several geysers. Geysers are like natural fountains, and the geysers on Enceladus spew out vast amounts of ice into outer space. It's a giant ice-water fountain, spraying out a frankly colossal amount of stuff into the cosmos! Makes our Niagara Falls less impressive.

WHO CAME BEFORE YOU?

You know, you won't be the first person to have bravely explored the great vastness of space. From the 1950s, humanity became obsessed with exploring the boundaries of our known Universe and launched several major space programs. If you're going to become an astronaut, great - but you need to first know what the pioneering astronauts of the last 80 years have already done.

Here are a few of the amazing discoveries already made by those giants who came before.

1. Sputnik and the first astronaut

The earliest journeys into space were successfully done by Russia in 1957. Russia and America were competing to see who had the best technology, and who could get to space first. For years, both countries had worked tirelessly on designing and building rockets that could launch into outer space. For years, both countries had failed to do so.

That is, until October 1957, when Russia launched *Sputnik*. This was a satellite that was launched using a rocket, and it remained in Earth's orbit and sent out beeps that could be heard using radios on Earth. America was gob-smacked. How had the Russians managed this? A further shock followed a month later when the first astronaut was launched into space aboard the *Sputnik II*. That astronaut was called Laika.

Laika was a dog. Yep! Laika the Dog was launched on the second-ever satellite and will go down in history as the greatest astronaut ever. Unfortunately, Laika didn't survive the journey but has been memorialized with a statue at Moscow in Russia.

2. The brave first human astronauts

So, a dog had gone into space, so what! You're not a dog, and they make pretty bad astronauts. It wasn't until 1961 that a human being was put into outer space, and that was a Russian (Russia again!) man called Yuri Gagarin.

Gagarin was launched on 12 April, and he completed one full orbit around Earth, which lasted 108 minutes. He said, "I could have gone on flying through space forever," and had experienced something that no one had ever done before.

Three weeks later, America managed to get an American into space. He was called Alan Shepard. Shepard didn't leave Earth for as long as Gagarin, taking a smaller flight of about 15 minutes, but it was still a massive moment for America. It was after this flight that America decided that they had to commit themselves to greater space exploration.

3. Just a short 238,855 miles!

The next step in space exploration seemed obvious. United States President John F. Kennedy announced in 1961, "I believe that this nation should commit itself to achieving the goal, of landing a man on the Moon and returning him safely to the Earth."

A tough challenge - after all the Moon is 238,855 miles away from Earth and is constantly moving!

Up until 1961, the only progress made toward *any* trip to the Moon was in 1959, when Russia launched *Luna 2*, which hit the Moon. It didn't have a human onboard, and it didn't make the return journey. NASA, the American space program, decided to dedicate itself to achieving President Kennedy's goal.

Throughout the 1960s, America developed as much technology as it could that might help with reaching the Moon. This was the quickest, most intense amount of work on space travel of all time. By the end of the 1960s, America believed that it was in a good position to succeed!

In 1968, Project Apollo was launched. Project Apollo was a series of flights between 1968 and 1972 that would bring humans into contact with the Moon. In 1968, a shuttle orbited the Moon with humans onboard and returned to Earth. In 1969, *Apollo 11* landed and the first people stepped out onto the Moon.

The first astronaut to do this was Neil Armstrong. As he disembarked from the craft, he famously said, "That's one small step for man, one giant leap for mankind." Apparently, this was a mistake. He meant to say, "One small step for *a* man," but was nervous and got it wrong. Regardless, it's still one of the most famous quotes of all time, and people continue to reference it to this day! You can even watch the Moon landing on YouTube!

4. The Voyager's seriously long voyages!

Following the success of the moon landings, NASA was desperate to continue to show off just how much it could do in space. Their next big move in space was to launch the *Voyager 1* and *Voyager 2* in 1977.

The *Voyagers* were probes that went on a mission to explore further than humans had ever gone before, and they're still out in space doing their work today. The Voyager probes collected information about Jupiter, Saturn, Uranus, Neptune, and the changing atmosphere in different parts of the Milky Way. NASA gathered a great deal of knowledge from the information sent back to Earth, and this mission's work is some of the most significant ever undertaken by human beings.

The probes each move more than 34,000 miles per hour, which would get you to the Moon in about six hours. They've been accelerating for over 45 years now and continue to drift further and further away from the humans that launched them. NASA estimates that the two probes will probably leave the Solar System, becoming the first known object to do so. They'll do this in about 14,000 years, however, so we may not be around to hear what they have to report back.

Perhaps the probes will one day be picked up by something other than a human…

5. The International Space Station

Unfortunately, across human history, there haven't been many times when people have just *worked together*. We don't tend to, not even in space travel. After all, Russia and America had been fighting over who was the best at it for years!

That is, until 1998, when the International Space Station was completed, marking the start of modern space exploration.

The International Space Station (ISS) is a large craft, weighing in at 990,000 lbs. It is visible from Earth in the right conditions and stays in Earth's orbit. It was constructed by five space agencies, America's *NASA*, Russia's *Roscosmos*, Japan's *JAXA*, Europe's *ESA*, and Canada's *CSA*.

The station remains in outer space constantly so that key scientific experiments can be carried out, testing the capabilities and limitations of humans in space. It has never come out of orbit and maintains a constant crew of astronauts and scientists, who change over throughout the year. It orbits the Earth quickly, completing about 15 orbits in an Earth Day, sitting 250 miles above the Earth's surface.

The ISS may be crucial for all space exploration in the future, and should any craft look to travel to Mars, it will probably have to do it from the ISS! Any astronaut would want a chance to float around the historic station's corridors and talk with the best and bravest the planet has to offer.

6. The Hubble Space Telescope

Have you ever had the chance to look through a telescope before? If you haven't then you must try to! Perhaps a neighbor has one, or a friend from school.

Telescopes enable us to see further than we can with our naked eye - much further. The earliest telescopes were invented in 1608 and were used to gaze at our galaxy for the first time.

Since then, technology has only improved, and in 1990, the most important telescope of all time was launched. That's right, *launched!*

The Hubble Space Telescope isn't a stationary telescope, operated by someone in their back garden. Instead, it orbits the Earth about 62 miles further out than the ISS.

Because the telescope isn't on Earth, it can take pictures without Earth's light and atmosphere affecting it too much. The Hubble Telescope can capture extremely high-resolution images as it gazes past our galaxy, and into deep space.

7. The roving Rovers

As you will be journeying to Mars, you should know whose footsteps you'll be following. Or rather, whose *wheels* you'll be following.

No human being has yet set foot on Mars. Instead, a series of vehicles have had a good roll around on the red planet in the name of science. These vehicles are called rovers. They look like tall buggies and have been roaming Mars since 1997, gathering amazing knowledge about the place.

There have been five so far, called: Sojourner, Spirit, Opportunity, Curiosity, and Perseverance. Schoolchildren came up with all the names (we're still waiting for NASA to allow Rover McRoverson).

The Rovers have cameras mounted on them that take hundreds and thousands of pictures as they roll about Mars. The pictures are sent back to Earth for scientists at NASA to analyze. They also take selfies with these cameras, for fun!

The Rovers are like little scientists themselves too. They can analyze rocks and soil better than any human on Earth. Using the information, scientists hope we can find out if Mars has ever had anything living on it before or *could* in the future.

So, when you eventually reach Mars, make sure you find the rovers and say hello. They've been a bit lonely since they left

Earth. Also, be careful with them - Perseverance has cost a whopping $2,800,000,000!

8. SpaceX

Space exploration is a darned expensive thing to do. This is why big organizations such as NASA exist; they're given billions and billions of dollars to help explore space, something that most of us will never be involved in.

Unless, of course, you also have billions and billions of dollars like the owner of Tesla, Elon Musk.

Elon Musk is known for having an eccentric personality and isn't afraid to invest his money in any project that he likes. This is why he set up the company SpaceX in 2002.

SpaceX aims to revolutionize space exploration, wanting to make the whole process easier and better. Since the company was founded, it has developed:

- *Reusable rockets.* This will make space travel so much cheaper as you don't have to make a brand-new rocket every single time you go to space!
- *The Starlink Project.* This project has launched hundreds of small satellites into Earth's orbit, possibly allowing access to high-speed internet from any part of the globe.
- *The Falcon Heavy.* This is a rocket that's capable of launching heavy goods into space with accuracy and

power. Did you know that, in 2018, to show off how good this rocket was, SpaceX launched a Tesla car into outer space? There'll be a confused alien on some faraway planet called *Zlorb* in 400 years wondering how to start it!

And there's more on the way! SpaceX is funded by one of the richest people in the world, who wants space to be accessible for future generations, and to help humans reach distances they've never reached before. Such as…

9. Space tourism

Most of us dream of going to outer space. We stare up at the dark night sky, picturing ourselves sitting in some space rocket while drinking a Diet Coke as stars whoosh past us at a speed that we can't even understand…

Strange as it is to think about, we're not far off of that dream, thanks to the work of SpaceX and Virgin!

Just as SpaceX is owned by a billionaire obsessed with space, Virgin is also owned by a billionaire obsessed with space! These two companies have been desperately competing to see which will be the first to send people into outer space for *fun*.

That's right, just for a laugh! No science is involved - just comfort, enjoyment, and relaxation. In 2023, Virgin tested its tourist space shuttles for the first time, with test civilians, and it faced no major problems. The idea is that you simply go for a relatively long journey into outer space, look at a few things, and then return home to tell everyone the story.

This is happening right now and will be available to the public within the next few years. The catch? Well, the catch is that it costs about $250,000 per ticket! You better start saving.

10. Space spiders? What next?

Laika may have been the first animal to be sent into orbit, but Laika certainly wasn't the last. Many animals have taken the voyage into outer space, usually for the benefit of a science experiment.

Scientists can study how space and zero gravity impact living organisms by taking animals to space, which might even help pave the way for future space travel innovations. Here are a few notable examples:

- *Ham the Chimp!* Ham was launched into space in 1961 and was the first 'humanoid' launched into space. His successful flight paved the way for safe human flight. A chimp was selected due to its remarkably close relationship with humans.
- *Fruit Flies.* If you've ever seen a fruit fly before, you may well have thought, "Oh gross," which is fair enough. But they have helped form a crucial study of life in zero

gravity. Fruit flies have a very short life span, so scientists took them into space to look at how zero gravity affected the full lives of flies. They observed uncommon behaviors, which helped them gain an understanding of how humans might hold up to long-term space travel.

- *Spiders.* Spiders were sent into space in the 1970s to see how they got on building their webs in outer space. The experiment helped scientists understand how space conditions impact basic functions in simple creatures.

This is just a small snapshot of the animals that have visited space. Why not look into some more research to find out even more for yourself?

BECOMING AN ASTRONAUT

So far, you've learned about the Solar System and the history of space travel. Don't you think it's about time that we get you out there?

Well, NASA doesn't just shove any old so-and-so up there, you know. Becoming an astronaut takes a lot of time, dedication, and smarts. Here's a guide on what steps to take to become an intrepid explorer of space.

1. Maybe you're born with it...

Being an astronaut is unfortunately not possible for every person. As an astronaut, you may need to spend a long time, days and weeks, in cramped and uncomfortable conditions. As such, you need to possess certain physical attributes:

- You must be between 5 feet, 2 inches and 6 feet, 3 inches in height. Any smaller or taller, and you'd struggle with getting around inside the spacecraft.
- You need perfect vision. Usually, people who require glasses and contact lenses aren't able to achieve perfect vision with these aids so wouldn't be allowed to go. Luckily, there is laser-eye surgery available if you're *really* desperate!
- You must weigh between 110 and 209 lbs. This is to ensure that extra fuel isn't wasted and that you're a healthy weight to cope with the physical demands of the job. Get running!

- Have good hearing. We can't have you shouting "eh!? Say that again, Houston!" down the communications line now, can we?

These are some of the main physical requirements for astronauts. You may naturally have disadvantages or advantages over others because of these, and some people are unfortunately disqualified straight away.

2. Stop talking in class

Listen here, you class clowns, hallway rebels, and lunchtime warriors! If you ever want to stand a chance of becoming a genuine space hero, you'll need to knuckle down and focus at school.

Astronauts achieve brilliant grades at school. In other words, they focus hard and do their very best from a young age. Those who pay close attention to mathematics and science will get themselves superb grades by the time they're looking to leave school. When it comes to deciding who should fly billions of dollars' worth of equipment in an environment that humans aren't supposed to be in, NASA won't choose the kid who got a C- in Math.

So, focus! It doesn't stop there either; budding astronauts get fantastic grades so they can do it all over again…

3. Start researching now

The road to becoming an astronaut is not easy! It takes years of hard work and lots of research. Most astronauts will give the same advice to children looking to become astronauts and that is to study straight away.

This means that you should try and learn as much as you can about space now!

Many astronauts recommend that you watch movies and documentaries about space, read books (like this one) on the subject, and in general try to *learn*.

Your school will be able to educate you on space but not nearly enough for a budding space explorer! You'll need to put the groundwork in early so that you don't have to do so much learning once you leave school and head to college.

4. Get a degree, or two; in fact, three can't hurt...

When you're done with your schooling, with loads of A grades and a pat on the back from the principal, there's more education to come.

Astronauts have to go to college and get themselves a degree.

Degrees are difficult qualifications that prove you're an expert in your subject. Astronauts will need to have spent at least four years gaining a degree, though many spend seven!

You can't go and just study anything, either. Astronauts have to get their degree in mathematics, computer science, engineering, or biological science. Basically, they're super smart.

To give you an idea of how qualified you can be as an astronaut, just look at the career of Jonathan Yong Kim. 'Jonny' is a Doctor of Medicine, has a degree in mathematics, was a sailor for the navy, and an astronaut. He managed to do all of this by the age of only 36!

5. "This is your captain speaking"

Once you've gained your difficult qualifications in Mathematics or Engineering or some such field, you may want to try your hand at getting a job for Hawaiian Airlines.

NASA has said that you don't *need* to do this to become an astronaut, but it's very beneficial and will help guarantee you the dream job.

Most astronauts spend 1,000 hours working as a pilot before they will even apply to work at NASA. It may be a long time to spend flying a passenger jet around the world, but the experience gained is crucial.

Astronauts will spend their time learning how to listen to commands and communicate with people outside of the craft. They also learn how to deal with difficult or unexpected problems, as well as how to *fly* a large craft.

It's generally considered best if you've been a pilot for the military or navy, but some pilots worked for civilian airlines. Neil Armstrong, the first man on the Moon, worked as an airline pilot, and he's the most famous astronaut of all time! So, before you get anywhere near a huge rocket, you'll be better off flying a planeload of American tourists to Paris first.

6. Learn Russian!

Вам придется научиться говорить по-русски, а не только по-английски. Если вы этого не сделаете, вас будут считать менее ценным. Тупой!

If you don't know what that means, then you're not ready to be an astronaut. Kind of.

It says, "You will have to learn to speak Russian, not just English. If you don't, you will be considered less valuable. Doofus!"

All astronauts are eventually provided with language training, but knowing both English and Russian will put you ahead. This is because some parts of the ISS (the International Space Station, see Chapter Two for more) use Russian while others use English.

As well as this, one of the shuttles that take astronauts into orbit is Russian-operated, so you'll want to know what they're saying.

Russian is a difficult language to learn if you're from an English-speaking country, but there's no getting around it! It simply isn't safe to have astronauts in orbit who may not be able to fix serious problems because they don't know the language.

So, learn this phrase at least, to help you get into the training:

Привет, я хочу быть космонавтом.
("Privet, ya khochu byt' kosmonavtom.")
("Hello. I'd like to be an astronaut.")

7. Get a gym membership!

Astronauts have to be healthy and fit. In Chapter Four, you'll see that astronauts are put under a great deal of physical stress when they do their jobs. Their bodies have to withstand massive amounts of force while they take off, and floating around the ISS can do strange things to the human body.

Space organizations also want to reduce the risk that something could go drastically wrong while an astronaut is in space. They won't take anyone who's at risk of heart attacks, strokes, or some other illness.

Because of all this, you'll have to be the right weight and in good shape to work as an astronaut.

So, while you learn Russian and study in your spare time, it might be worth running up and down the 100m track a few times after school. Or perhaps joining a sports team. Or a gymnastics class. Or all of them!

It's a good idea to make a routine of exercising while you're a child or teenager regardless of your space plans. Those who do will find it easier to stay fit and healthy when they're older, helping to stave off illness in old age.

8. Work on your people skills

Being an astronaut is an incredible experience and is a job that only a tiny fraction of humans will ever have the chance to do. However, some parts of it can *suck*. The main parts are the spacecraft themselves.

When you're provided with a mission by NASA or any other organization, you may spend months and months completing that mission. This means that you will spend months and months with the same people, in a *tiny*, enclosed spacecraft with no one else for company.

It doesn't matter if you've studied since you were three years old, have several amazing qualifications, and go to the gym every other hour…, if you're *annoying* then you're not going to be an astronaut!

Bob Thirsk was a Canadian astronaut who hired many people to become astronauts themselves. He said that he asked himself something very important before he'd offer a job to anyone:

"Would I enjoy spending a long period of time..., with this person? If I can say yes, I will go on and consider that person as a potential candidate."

So, you'll need to work on your 'people skills.' This means how you interact with other people. If you're argumentative or irritating, try to work on being a bit more chilled out or calm so you don't end up annoying your colleagues while you are thousands of miles away from home.

9. "Can I have a job, please?"

If you get to stage 9 of this chapter and can confidently say, "Yup! I can do all of that," then you're ready to apply for a job as an astronaut! Take a moment to celebrate your success and realize that you're unfortunately not over the finish line just yet.

Applying for a job can be a long, boring process in any profession, and it's the same for astronauts.

The first reason is that there isn't always a job for 'an astronaut' around. Space organizations have limited money, so don't hire people all the time. This means that much of your time will be spent searching every space program around the world to see who wants an astronaut.

Next, you write up a long application. This will involve answering hundreds of questions and writing a lot about how much you want to be an astronaut and why you'll be amazing at doing it.

Then you have to wait and hope that they pick you out of all of the applicants. In 2017, Canada had over 3,700 applicants to become an astronaut - and they only needed two!

If you then get chosen, there'll be tests of your knowledge, ability, and fitness. They'll also likely conduct interviews with your family and friends about the type of person you are and whether you've got any skeletons in the closet.

Then after all this...

Whoa. You don't get selected...

10. Don't give up

The last, and most important part of your quest to become an astronaut is not to give up. It takes years of work and dedication to be as qualified as you need to be, and even then, you may not get the job!

The trick is to not give up on trying. Keep on applying for the jobs, and keep on becoming the better candidate for the job.

Continue your education, gain relevant experience, conduct experiments, and work at yourself to help to achieve your goal.

Astronauts are naturally ambitious and want to be an astronaut at all costs. You'll have to be the same. There will be setbacks and problems along the way, but you must keep a cool head and try not to let it get you down. Life is all about the highs and lows. You may be failing to be an astronaut today, and tomorrow hired to conduct science experiments on the International Space Station. Who knows how it will all pan out?

You simply have to keep trying.

LEARNING TO FLY

So, you've put in the years of dedication required to become an astronaut, and congratulations, you've been selected by NASA! You're going to become one of the very few humans who get to journey into the terrifying emptiness of space.

We now come to the exciting part of this whole journey, starting your pathway with learning to become an astronaut. Astronauts have to go through the most highly-specialized and intense training in the world. It's not just obvious stuff either, astronauts aren't just pinged into outer space and told to 'get on with it.' No, no.

Astronauts run space missions that cost billions of dollars and might one day discover something that could help change the course of humanity forever. So, they have to be well trained. In this chapter, learn about ten of the most bizarre and fun aspects of astronaut training that you must undertake before you journey toward Mars.

1. Basic training

The first part of training for an astronaut is actually a package of lessons that are called 'basic training.'

This may sound simple, but it's anything but! Basic training takes two years to complete and is made up of a series of intense and grueling tasks.

Some of the basic training will involve astronauts piloting NASA's fleet of T-38 supersonic jets to gain piloting experience before they learn how to operate the complicated machinery onboard the ISS. They'll then learn how to perform dangerous spacewalks (where they perform tasks outside of the spaceship) in a 60-foot-deep swimming pool.

Astronauts also learn advanced Russian, how to use robotic arms on the ISS, how to operate a space station, extreme survival training, and complicated geography lessons. By the end of the two years, astronauts can survive with next to no supplies, identify aspects of rocks, and work the most complicated machinery ever constructed. Not bad.

2. Swimming to space

Bizarrely, a completely necessary part of learning how to be in space is learning how to swim. Sorry to those readers who shudder at the thought of the ocean, but you'll have to secure a few swimming badges at your local pool before you'll be allowed into a craft.

During an astronaut's first month of training, they must pass an exhausting swimming test.

The new explorers must swim three full lengths of a swimming pool. That's 82 yards! Oh, and did we mention that they'll do all of this while wearing shoes and a full-flight suit (with helmet) that weighs over 280 lbs.?

The astronauts are allowed to do this as slowly or quickly as they like; there's no time limit. They can breaststroke, sidestroke, or freestyle their way through the exercise, but they'd better make sure that some energy is still in the tank. Once they've finished swimming, the astronauts must tread water for ten minutes straight.

That's a lot of swimming! Some astronauts are very surprised at the amount of swimming they must quickly learn, and some struggle to pass this particular skill. So, if you sink rather than swim, maybe it's time to do some practice in your local pool now before you get to NASA.

3. Arizona's practice moon

Picture the Moon and think carefully about its surface. The moon is covered in craters. Craters are large, circular pits that can form for a variety of reasons. It may be that small meteorites hit them and left the pit behind, or there's been some other natural cause that led to the strange feature.

Well, as the Moon is currently the only place in space that humans have set foot on, it's seen as a good idea to train astronauts in how to navigate craters.

Earth has plenty of craters all over the place, meteorites have smacked into our planet for literally millions of years. The problem is that there's nowhere on Earth with such an abundance of craters similar to those found on the Moon. You can't just tell your astronauts to drive around *one* crater - they'll never learn anything!

So, NASA directors chose Arizona to be the destination for a 'practice moon' so astronauts could learn to navigate the Moon's surface. There was already a large meteorite crater there, so it seemed only right. In 1963, geologists decided to plant a load of dynamite all around the crater for miles around, and then blew it all up.

The result was a large piece of terrain that looks - and feels - like the Moon's surface. Astronauts now drive large rovers around the area to test how to control the bulky vehicles when navigating huge craters.

4. The vomit comet

When a person goes into outer space, they escape from the force of gravity. When this happens, they achieve something known as 'weightlessness.' Weightlessness means that everything will float around completely free from gravity and behave strangely. Therefore, astronauts need to know how to deal with this, so they don't freak out.

So, how do we achieve weightlessness without going into space?

Well, either you can lower people into one of the *massive* swimming pools that NASA has, which does a pretty good job, or you can use a special plane.

In 1959, NASA worked with the U.S. Air Force to theorize a plane that could achieve actual weightlessness for astronauts to practice in. Ex-military planes, capable of extremely fast speeds, were adapted by the air force, and they began to develop the lovely 'vomit comet.'

A vomit comet is a wide plane that's been fitted with padded walls (for safety) and a large area where many people can stand freely. The plane is then flown in a "~~" sort of motion. A wavey, up-and-down way. This means the plane constantly goes on sharp inclines and rapid drops. If done correctly then the people inside will experience about 20–25 seconds of weightlessness on the drops.

NASA estimates that one in three people vomit the first time that they undertake this unnerving training. While it's unpleasant, it's better that they do so on the plane instead of all over an important control panel thousands of miles away from the Earth's surface!

5. Toilet time

Tim Peake, a crew member of the International Space Station was once asked how you go to the toilet in space. He responded:

"Carefully."

In space, nothing acts as it does on Earth. When you visit the toilet on Earth, gravity does a helpful job of making sure that all of your waste *drops* into the bowl before being taken away by a rush of water. The problem is that, in space, where there's no gravity, this would lead to an almighty mess of water, toilet paper, and flying poop. So, it's necessary to teach astronauts how to go to the toilet.

The toilets onboard space vessels are operated using vacuum suction, like a very expensive vacuum cleaner. The toilet has a hose that attaches, actively sucking away the gross-ness, before sealing it in a storage container (and, no we can't just shoot urine into outer space - what if it hits an alien?)

The difficulty comes when an astronaut needs to go number two. The vacuum's opening is about four inches across, which is about a third smaller than the average toilet. To avoid a big mistake, these clever astronauts must aim their poop very, very well.

So, practice makes perfect, as well as making sure your space suit remains dry and stench-free.

6. Giant game of air hockey, anyone?

The great thing about zero gravity, other than being able to fly, is that *all* objects lose their weight. This means that you could easily lift a fully grown elephant above your head…, provided it was a polite elephant. So, astronauts can move really heavy objects without much effort. That is unless the object is already moving.

If an object is moving, it will continue to do so without stopping, until something *makes* it stop. This means that if you push a large, metal chair in the ISS, it's going to continue at the same speed that it set off at, forever, until it hits something. This can be dangerous onboard a spaceship, so astronauts need to practice how to carefully control objects and how to *stop* them as well.

How do we do this? You can't use the vomit comet this time! So, NASA came up with an ingenious solution. They decided to create an air hockey *room*.

Inside a large room in the Johnson Space Center, a floor has been developed that is almost perfectly level, highly polished, and super-smooth. Objects are then put on top of special pads that create an air cushion between the floor and the object. The effect of this is that objects move around the floor with next to no contact with the floor.

Astronauts practice on this floor, which NASA calls a giant air hockey table. They push objects around and learn how to stop things from simply speeding away from them at a tremendous speed. Or they don't, and Larry the Janitor is furious when yet another chair tips over his cart.

7. Centrifugal barf

This next one is a bit confusing, and a bit vomit-inducing.

When an object is getting faster, it's doing something called *accelerating*. When something accelerates slowly, we don't tend to notice it too much. Our bodies adjust to the small amount of acceleration. Think about being in a car that quickly speeds up to overtake another car. You get a bit of an odd feeling in your stomach, but all is well.

The quicker that acceleration happens, the greater the effect is on the accelerating thing and the human inside of it.

A space shuttle has to quickly reach speeds of 17,500 miles per hour. It accelerates quicker than any other human-made vehicle. The amount of force that astronauts experience during this is *serious*.

Astronauts must somehow get used to this level of acceleration and force. Human beings can easily become unconscious during strong acceleration; people might also vomit, something that's not advisable in a space suit helmet. To practice this, astronauts take trips in something called a *centrifuge*.

Centrifuges are basically big spinning things that spin extremely fast. Positioned in a pod attached to a powerful centrifuge, astronauts experience a huge amount of acceleration, and similar forces to a space flight can be simulated. Astronauts use centrifuges to help their bodies get used to coping with the crazy amounts of speeds that they'll have to deal with when they launch into outer space.

8. Strengthening the will

There's no way of pretending that space travel is fun. Astronauts spend a long time in extreme environments, separated from all other humans on Earth. It's completely unnatural for human beings to do that, and it could do horrible things to their minds.

This started with the Russians. They were the first to create space missions that lasted six months in the 1970s. Their missions had to be abandoned before they were finished because the astronauts were going mad with the isolation.

NASA and Russia worked together on a space mission called *Mir*, which allowed the organizations to learn about long-duration missions and the effect they could have on astronauts. Psychologists analyzed the behavior of the unfortunate volunteers, who reported that, after months of living in space, they were feeling awful and struggling.

Astronauts are now given intense psychological training before their mission. They typically know that they're going to go into space about two years before they do so. The astronauts spend some of the two years with expert psychologists and doctors who help them prepare for their long journey. The astronauts are taught how to remain calm, how to keep control of their emotions, and how to deal with isolation.

Astronauts are also given relaxation help on spaceships. They're provided with music, television, movies, games, or books to help keep their minds occupied when they're not busy conducting vital research.

At the end of the day, it's not normal for human beings to be so far away from Earth, so it's bound to take its toll. It's just as important to take care of the brain as it is to take care of the body.

9. Run away!

The worst fear for anyone involved in space programs is that something seriously wrong will happen with a spacecraft while it's *in* space. If a fire breaks out, or there's a breach in the craft, the most essential thing to do is to try to save the astronauts' lives. Because of this, they have to undertake *Emergency Egress Training*.

Emergency Egress basically means, "There's an emergency, get out now."

Astronauts are put into extreme environments to practice this emergency egress. They might be placed in a fake spacecraft underwater or in high-altitude locations. They then have to go through highly complex emergency procedures that are focused on getting them out of the craft as quickly as possible and as safely as possible.

This is the training that all astronauts hope they never have to use. But there have been catastrophic problems onboard spacecraft before, and there may be some more in the future. It's crucial to give astronauts every chance to survive a serious emergency.

10. Waiting

The most common thing that astronauts do during their training is *waiting*.

A team of astronauts may very well be assigned to a mission ("Congratulations, you're visiting the Moon!"), but it will take years for that mission to actually be carried out. For all of that time, astronauts are standing by, waiting and learning.

It's not all just sitting around, eating sandwiches, and flying planes. They're going through very specific training for their mission, preparing to become heroes.

Some astronauts don't even get a mission after their training, however. They may have years to wait without a promise of a future mission to keep them going. Those lucky individuals spend their time working at NASA, completing science projects and assignments that may need work here on Earth.

Either way, if you want to be the world's best astronaut, you'll have to put in your time waiting and twiddling your thumbs first.

HOUSTON, WE HAVE LIFT-OFF!

We're now at the halfway point of the book, and we're about to go INTO SPACE! This chapter is all about the 'lift-off' - the moment that a colossal rocket is launched into the vast cosmos, with you onboard.

This is an intensely difficult and precise part of space travel. Scientists have spent decades trying to work out the safest way of launching a rocket into space. You're going to have thousands of gallons of fuel strapped to your shuttle and set on fire. The forces that you'll feel will only be felt by 0.00001% of people ever, and the chance of an instant explosion is not exactly small!

This chapter will tell you what happens when you lift off. You'll start the chapter on planet Earth and end it some thousands of miles outside of it, getting ready to head to Mars.

1. If you fail to plan, then you plan to fail!

The most pivotal part of launching a rocket into outer space comes far before the rocket even exists. The reason that it takes years for an astronaut to reach space is because of all the planning that has to happen first.

NASA can't just say, "Yep, we'll put Terry in space. Go get a big rocket from the Big Rocket Store and we'll do it next Monday." It takes so much thinking and work from scientists, space agencies, and engineers to work out the whole mission first.

Multiple things must be considered. Firstly, the space agency decides what the aims of the mission will be, how long it's going to go on, and who is going. Then the scientists work out what type of space shuttle is going to be required, what expertise the astronauts need, and what needs to go into outer space to help the mission succeed. Finally, the engineers work extremely hard to figure out what type of rocket to build, what space shuttle to construct, and how they're going to get them into outer space.

This takes months to figure out and then years to construct. It may not be exciting for you, the astronaut, but these are the important meetings that mean you don't explode within two seconds!

2. "Can I have it in green?"

The next bit is the creation of the rocket, which is incredible.

When you are launched into space, you won't be doing it in the rocket. You'll be on board a space shuttle, which is attached *to* the rocket. Rockets are vehicles that have multiple parts or stages that activate at different times. Each stage or part has its own separate function, engines, and fuel.

The design and construction of the rocket are incredibly exciting. The engineer needs to make sure that the different stages happen in the correct order, that the right amount of fuel is ordered, and crucially, that it goes the right way up.

Yep, you heard that right. If a rocket is the *tiniest* bit wrong in its orientation, or design, then your space shuttle may not go the right direction. It could end up spinning, or twisting in the air, which can have catastrophic consequences! The engineers must get everything right. There's simply no room for error. You'll be hoping and praying you had a good one in charge of this Mars project when you're sitting in the cockpit. Just don't think too much about that loose screw you saw as you took your seat…

3. Pre-launch preparations

Okay, we're getting close to launching, promise. The next part is the 'getting it all ready' section. It's called the "pre-launch preparations," and it's like putting the jigsaw together. The space shuttle is attached to the rocket, and all the systems are checked again and again and again. If there's a single thing wrong, it's best to know now, and not when you're two months closer to Mars!

If all the systems check out, then the fuel is loaded into each part of the rocket. The fuel will have been worked out precisely. The mission needs exactly enough for the mission, no more and no less. If the rockets and shuttle are overloaded with fuel, then the whole project will be overweight, leading to all calculations being inaccurate. The fuel will be triple-checked, then checked once more before having one last look…, and then it will be loaded.

The checks will not stop until you're already lifting off. Every single physical mechanism and computer function is tested repeatedly to make sure it will do what it needs to. Amazingly, we're a third of the way through the whole 'lift-off' section, and the astronaut isn't even in a space suit yet. Hopefully, you see why this long process is so important.

4. Countdown

Finally, we're now into the countdown, the part of the launch where the world listens in with bated breath, gazing into their television screens as they listen to the NASA command center count down to the rocket launch:

"10...9...8...7...6...5...4...3..."

Except we're not *there* yet.

The countdown doesn't happen ten seconds before the rocket launches. It actually starts about two days or so before we get to that. The *Artemis I*, which launched on November 16, 2022, had a countdown of precisely 47 hours and 40 minutes.

The countdown is worked out a long way in advance. The countdown details exactly when certain checks are carried out, when certain teams arrive to work and when they leave, when things are turned on and when they're turned off and when you poop - everything! (Okay, not the poop bit).

The countdown is precise and has no room for error. Every single member of the team must do their job exactly when instructed to make sure that the mission happens when it is supposed to. The whole countdown is called "L minus," which shows how far away from lift-off we are in hours and minutes. "T minus" is closer to the launch. "T" is 'time,' which just means when we're going to launch. For Artemis I, "T minus" was only the last ten minutes!

Okay, now you can have the famous countdown. Say it out loud in your most dramatic voice:

"TEN...NINE...EIGHT...SEVEN...SIX...FIVE...FOUR...

THREE...TWO...ONE...WE HAVE LIFT-OFF!"

5. Ignition

The countdown has finished; the crew is aboard their shuttle and now comes the scariest part of the whole liftoff procedure. Ignition.

Ignition means setting something on fire. Here, the fuel is what's being set on fire. The rocket's engines ignite, and they create a colossal amount of thrust. Huge, billowing clouds of smoke erupt from the rear of the rocket and a jet of dragon-like fire blasts into the ground. The rocket begins to shake and tremble under the pressure of the explosion happening at its rear.

Slowly, the rocket rises from the ground as the thrust overpowers gravity, and the crew ascends into the sky. The engines continue to generate a crazy amount of energy and power. The astronauts experience the pull of gravity inside the cockpit. There's a chance that some will pass out even after all their training; the rest are just waiting for the launch to be finished.

There have been cases of an instant explosion at ignition. Getting through this stage without any complications is a good sign. You're on your way...

6. Escaping Earth

This whole procedure is all about getting away from Earth's gravitational pull. If the engines cut out, or we lose fuel too fast, then the rocket will lose thrust and gravity will pull it back to Earth (which we don't want).

The rocket will have to continuously produce massive amounts of power until it breaks free from the Earth's atmosphere, a ring around the planet that marks the end of gravity's control. Once the rocket is out of the atmosphere, it has reached space. On board the vessel, you will be spoken to by ground control. They attempt to tell you how the launch is going and inform you that you're breaking through the bounds of Earth, and into space.

7. Watch out below!

Do you remember when we mentioned earlier that rockets have many parts or stages? Well, this is their time to shine.

The first-stage rocket has propelled you into the air, accelerating away from the launchpad at an incredible speed. As the rocket accelerates away from Earth and every living human, then, the first stage runs out of fuel. Ground control informs the astronauts onboard that the first-stage rocket is now being 'jettisoned.' This means it's being let go. Hopefully not into someone's backyard.

As this happens, the second-stage rocket kicks in and continues pushing the rocket into outer space. This rocket will have an easier task, however, because the weight has reduced thanks to Mr. First Stage's departure. This will continue through the stages until the final stage is reached, which is by far the most vital one.

8. The final stage

The final stage engine is crucial, and its purpose differs with every mission. If NASA is launching a craft that needs to be in Earth's orbit, then the final stage engine will fire just enough to put the craft into orbit and no further. The spacecraft will be at the perfect speed and will slot into orbit quite happily. Earth's orbit has force to it, so will keep objects in its orbit provided they're not going too fast.

However, you're not staying in Earth's orbit. Your job is to go to Mars. In this instance, the final-stage engine needs to fire at the right time and with the right amount of power to propel the craft out of Earth's orbit, on a course to Mars.

This has to be pretty exact. The space shuttle will have the ability to correct its course, but the final stage needs to set you on the right course and at a suitable speed for the mission to be a success. It can't launch you off at a ridiculous speed that will send you through Mars' orbit, it has to be just right.

"Those engineers better have got this right!" You'll think as you escape Earth's orbit and begin your journey toward Mars (and hopefully no further).

9. Payload deployment

All has gone well! The final-stage engine has set you on a course toward Mars, and all is looking good. The other astronauts have finished vomiting, and they're able to begin their mission.

At this point, the spacecraft separates from the final stage, leaving it behind. The engine may stay in orbit for some time before it re-enters Earth's atmosphere and likely burns to a crisp. From here, the space shuttle holding the astronauts is in charge of its own destiny, NASA got you into space, now go and do your job.

If the mission also involves putting some satellites into Earth's orbit, then now's the time to do that. They'll be released with the final stage, and they'll spin around the Earth, carrying out their own mission.

10. Mission time

That's it. Lift-off is intense, and NASA has had many missions fail during lift-off. So much care is put into the process because so much can go wrong. The important thing is that it didn't go wrong for you!

The ground control team will be celebrating a successful flight. For some of the scientists and engineers on planet Earth, this will be the biggest moment in their lives. The coming together of years and years of research, late nights, and thankless work.

Ground control will continue to talk to you throughout your journey. They might transmit video messages to your shuttle from your family and friends, keep you up-to-date on any reports they get in, and listen to your findings. Ground control is the only link to planet Earth that you have from here, so hopefully the communication technology stays active.

Launches are only possible because everyone works together. They're beautiful moments when they go right. It's a true indication of how far we humans have come. Once upon a time, we were fashioning spears out of rocks, now you're on your way to Mars...

Humans Go Weird in Space

The world gasped, screamed, and cheered as your space shuttle left the planet, sending you on your way to Mars. Congratulations, you and your team are about to become the loneliest human beings of all time! You're also about to put your body through conditions that it's just not supposed to go through.

HUMANS GO WEIRD
IN OUTER SPACE

1. Weightlessness

We've already spoken about weightlessness in this book. If you missed it, then re-read Chapter Four!

Ultimately, almost everything that you read about in this chapter happens because of the lack of gravity. We're made for planet Earth and its gravity, not for space with its ZERO gravity. Simply put, humans go weird in space. This chapter will tell you about some of the strange effects that space has on animals that were supposed to stay on planet Earth.

You know by now that when you leave Earth, you escape its gravity. When this happens, you'll float about and experience something known as weightlessness. You'll bob around the ship, with no weight. "Boring!" You say, "I know this already!" Fair enough, but it's not just *you* that will experience weightlessness, you know.

Everything on your ship will now behave weirdly because of zero gravity, and that can have some funky results.

Most importantly, liquids will act in a way that is almost impossible to see on Earth. Liquid floats in zero gravity, as large spherical blobs. This means that astronauts can't just chug some water out of a bottle. Instead, they have to use straws and special packets; otherwise, the water would escape and splash around in their ship!

This can also have strange effects on your tears. Astronaut Chris Hadfield recorded a video that you can watch on YouTube, showing what happens when you cry in space. While on Earth, your tears cascade down your face onto your cheeks. In space, the tears bubble up into your eyes again and then float away as little blobs.

It'll take some serious getting used to, but eventually, you'll master drinking, crying, and urinating in zero gravity. Might be a bit of a mess to clean up after the first few times is all.

2. What's the time?

Time is one of those things that just gets more complicated, the more you know. You know what time is, it's how we divide up the day and how we know roughly when we need to be awake, and when to sleep.

Our bodies get used to this routine very quickly. We use our understanding of time to dictate what we do and when, and that is based on the rising and setting of the Sun. The only reason that the Sun sets and rises on Earth, is because Earth is spinning. What happens when you're no longer on Earth?

Well, the Sun never sets. You never have a natural day or night. This can cause havoc with your sleep schedule, and astronauts can end up sleeping at random times unless they're very careful. This might sound like it's not much of an inconvenience, but if the crew doesn't stay in sync, then you end up with a very dysfunctional team!

Keep an eye on your crewmates, and make sure you're sleeping and waking at the same time. Sleep is key - humans are stupid without sleep.

3. Burritos taste like feet now!

Eating is really important to people; we have to consume food to keep up our happiness levels. There's a reason that the word *hangry* was added to the dictionary in 2018! (Hangry means that you're angry because you're hungry).

This is equally essential while you're in space. Mealtimes become one of the times of the day that everyone looks forward to. You get to sit down with your workmates, have a chat, and enjoy a delicious meal to reward you for your hard work. The problem is that you may not know if it's actually delicious at all.

This is because your sense of taste and smell is dramatically altered in space. Astronauts regularly report that food doesn't taste so strongly while they're in space, and some people almost entirely lose their ability to taste at all.

This is because, when you go into space, your bodily fluids become affected by the lack of gravity. On Earth, they're pulled downward, toward your legs, but in space, they float around wherever they please. This leads to the liquid going toward your head and can make you have a very puffy, swollen face. All this fluid blocks your nasal passages, and you lose your ability to smell properly. It's like having a very heavy cold.

Smell and taste are very closely linked, so when you lose your ability to smell, your taste is impacted. To get over this, astronauts bring strong-tasting condiments to put on their food, so that they can taste anything about their meal. NASA makes sure to stow BBQ sauce, hot sauce, soy sauce, and honey so the astronauts can add some flavor if they need it.

What condiment or sauce are you going to make sure they add to your flight?

4. Muscle atrophy

Human beings use their muscles all the time. As you move, you use muscles and strengthen them. Some humans like to spend their time in gyms, working their bodies as hard as they can so they can develop the biggest and best muscles. Good on them!

The problem in space is that you're not going to be using your muscles a lot of the time. Weightlessness makes many tasks easy to perform, so you'll hardly be working out your body at all on a normal day. In fact, the tasks take so little physical effort, that you can experience something called *muscular atrophy*.

This means that your muscles will deteriorate over time, becoming smaller and less effective because they're not being used. Astronauts have to keep up intense levels of exercise to stop this from happening. On board the ISS, astronauts take part in two-and-a-half hours of training and exercise daily to combat muscular atrophy.

So, keep movin' - otherwise, you'll wither away by the time you get back to Earth!

5. Better in than in!

Of course, the saying is actually 'better out than in,' but that will not apply in space.

'Better out than in' means that it's always better to let something out of your body, rather than to leave it in. This usually refers to a loud, long, smelly burp!

Unfortunately, in space, you'll struggle to burp at all. Carbonated or fizzy drinks have lots of gas in them that rises through the liquid as bubbles on Earth. In space, no forces act on the liquid, so the bubbles don't behave normally; the gas just sits in the liquid.

This also means that the gas doesn't rise when it's in your tummy. If you have a soda on Earth, the gas rises, and your body feels the need to burp to release some gas out of your mouth. As this doesn't happen in space, drinking a soda can be really uncomfortable in space, and even painful.

An Australian company has developed a beer that they think could be safe to drink on flights. It's called Stout Space Beer and has very few bubbles in it. We'll just have to wait for Coca-Cola to come out with Coke Zero Bubbles!

6. Can you see the problem here?

This one is a serious issue for astronauts. If we don't figure out how to solve it, this problem will continue to limit the types of missions that humans can do.

In weightless conditions, the human eyeball does something strange. It *squashes*. Not dramatically - it doesn't turn into jelly or anything - but it does squash slowly over time, leading to the ball changing shape. Some astronauts come home with a flat back of the eyeball, and it can lead to a blurry vision for those affected. If you already suffer from nearsightedness, then you'll experience an improvement in your vision.

For some, however, the nerves in their eyes actually swell up in weightlessness. This is due to the fluids that we mentioned earlier. This can be really serious and can cause blindness if not immediately treated on Earth.

So, pay attention to your vision, and make sure to double-check that you're flying to Mars and not toward the Sun.

7. Swallowing in self-pity

A key part of being a human is in our swallowing. If you think about it, our ability to swallow means that we can drink water, eat food and keep a healthy cycle of liquids going through our body. It's pretty useful.

So, what happens if swallowing becomes incredibly difficult and, at times, impossible?

In space, the lack of gravity means that swallowing becomes incredibly challenging. Astronauts have to work on new and innovative techniques to help them drink and eat. If you're heading to Mars, then maybe work on some strange ways to swallow while you're eating dinner. Don't start trying to swallow like a lizard while you're out for dinner, though. The server will look at you funny.

8. Standing taller

Some people are quite concerned about their height. For many of us, it's not really a consideration, but many people wish that they could be *a bit* taller. Just a few inches!

Well, if that is something that you have always wanted, congratulations, it's going to happen on your trip to Mars.

The gravity on Earth compresses your body slightly. When this force is no longer happening, your bones aren't pushed together or compressed. Because of this, you grow by a few inches in space! It's not a huge difference, but it would be noticeable. Unfortunately, it doesn't last forever; after a small amount of time on Earth, you'll be back to your normal height.

Gravity holds us back from all being gigantic, long creatures, stalking the landscape. Just think how tall we could be without it!

9. Long-term sickness

Something you'll have to come to terms with is that space can give you serious illnesses that might endanger your life. Astronauts have to acknowledge that the longer they spend in space, the more likely this becomes.

When you go into space, you're traveling closer to the Sun, and further from Earth's protection. The Sun produces something called radiation, which can cause a very serious illness known as cancer.

Cancer is unfortunately an illness that kills a lot of animals and people on Earth, and Earth's atmosphere does its best to protect us from the Sun's radiation (this is why you must wear sun cream). When you're in your space shuttle, you'll be closer to the big fiery ball of radiation, and so you'll increase your chances of developing some serious health complications later in life.

It's not a fun side effect of space travel, but it's something worth thinking about…

10. Sleep, shmeep

The average person needs approximately eight hours of sleep a night. That varies between adults, teenagers, and children, but it's about eight hours. If you sleep more than that, then that's good. Sleep is good for people, and you should seek to have a healthy amount of it.

Good news! In space, astronauts have the comfiest sleep that any human could ever have, so you'll get lots of it…, is what we'd type if we were lying.

Astronauts have really poor sleep while in space. On average, astronauts just about achieve six hours of sleep a night, and many nights are worse than that. There's neither a clever nor science answer to this. The fact is that sleeping onboard a space shuttle is not easy. The beds are the best we can fit the shuttle with, and they're not cozy double beds!

Often astronauts share their sleeping quarters with other astronauts, and their mattresses are thin and uncomfortable. So, you toss and turn, trying to find a good sleeping spot and listening to the whirring of the shuttle - all while dealing with your crewmate's farts!

It's stinks, but it's a sacrifice you'll have to make to get to Mars. Get used to being sleepy.

WHAT WILL YOU
DO IN SPACE?

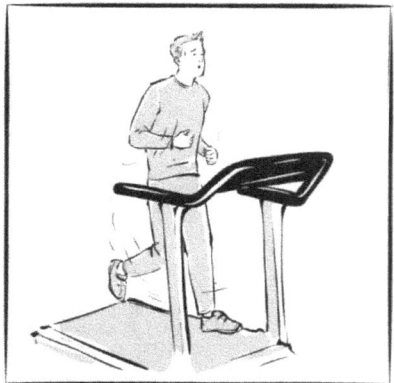

The average distance to Mars is 140 million miles, and it will take you about seven months to get there. You'll spend seven months onboard a space shuttle with some of the most talented scientists and engineers that the world has ever seen. What do you think you're going to do? Play video games and watch movies?

Well, maybe. This chapter is about what astronauts do in space, impossible distances away from life back home. Some of the points here are about the *job*, while some are more optional. But NASA isn't spending billions of dollars to throw you to another planet without keeping you busy. Every second is money when you're on this mission...

1. Evil science experiments...or just normal science experiments

Most astronauts are scientists. They studied for years to become a Doctor of Science, and they will have spent most of their life waiting to go into space for a reason. That reason is to discover something *new* about space, and the way to do that is through science.

Before you go into space, NASA will have brought together a group of scientists to help you decide what scientific experiments should be carried out. In this instance, you're going to Mars! There'll be lots to look at when you're there, but you're also going to travel through atmospheres and parts of the Solar System that we've never been to before.

What you'll discover on this mission will probably be some of the most unique findings that astronauts have ever come across. Much of your time will be spent being a proper scientist and trying to discover something new about the Universe.

2. Spacewalks

Spacewalks are something that, for some people, might just be the most terrifying thing imaginable. We touched on them briefly in Chapter Four, but there's a lot to discuss and to think about (because you very well may have to perform one!).

Spacewalks are also known as EVAs (Extravehicular Activities). These are tasks done by astronauts outside of the spacecraft. This means the astronaut puts themself into a huge space suit, attaches two cables to the suit, and drifts in open space. If, for some reason, both of the cables that hold you to the ship snapped, then you'd literally drift off into open space, with no hope of rescue.

So, yes, not for everyone.

But EVAs are important. EVAs are performed for a variety of tasks, a common one being to fix things on the outside of the ship. Repairing the outside of the ship, or something that's located there, might be crucial to your survival. If there's a life-support machine that's damaged then someone must get out there and fix it! While it may be a bit scary, you'll get used to walking into outer space with nothing to stop your never-ending tumble into the abyss, except for a high-tech bit of rope.

3. Daily regimen

While this isn't the most exciting part of space travel, it's still worth mentioning as it will take up the majority of your time onboard the spacecraft.

You have a daily regimen on Earth. This is essentially what you do every day. For most people that will include some hygiene, such as a shower or bath, going to the toilet, brushing teeth, sleeping, and exercising. 'Daily Regimen' is just a fancy phrase for 'living life.'

As well as these quite normal tasks, just like on Earth, astronauts might also find time to engage in activities such as watching a movie or reading a book. It can't all be science experiments and floating water, you know!

4. Communicating with home

Earlier in this book, we discussed how crucial it is to keep astronauts sane and happy on their mission. Entertainment and food play a major part in this, but astronauts also need to be able to contact home. This happens semi-regularly for many reasons.

Most astronaut contact with Earth is carried out via Mission Control, which is the base from which your mission will be observed. At any time, there will be someone there who can intervene in case of an emergency or receive contact from your vessel. There are regular, scheduled conversations with Mission Control, where updates are given on the mission or instructions are given over. It's also a great time to ask about something that you can't figure out, like how to get Corporal Jones back into the ship after his EVA cable snapped.

Other than calling home about work, astronauts also talk to their families by video chat. Think of it as a Solar System FaceTime. They don't get to do this whenever they want, but it gives those on the ship a chance to blow off steam, hear about any stories or updates from Earth, and just catch up with their family. It takes seven months to get to Mars, and another seven to get back...you'll want to hear from someone back home every so often.

5. Winning photography prizes

Since the first camera was invented in the 19th century, it's fair to say that people love a good picture. We, humans, have hundreds upon thousands of photography competitions all over the world. Winners of such competitions usually have captured a magnificent lion hunting on the plains of Africa, an interaction between primates in the jungle, or just maybe a gorgeous landscape shot of Hawaii.

Or, of course, an astronaut takes a picture and wins it every time.

Let's face it, what picture beats a real-life, genuine picture of outer space? Astronauts are given exceptional cameras to video and photograph everything that they encounter. Video cameras may be constantly rolling, but the photographs that are taken by astronauts could be just as crucial to some scientific understanding of the Universe. Sometimes, it's just a selfie though.

6. 'Hopefully, it's just a cold!'

Do you happen to know where the *worst* place to be sick is?

Yup, space.

Being ill or injured in space is inconvenient for everyone involved. And you very well may get sick. Bacteria survive very well in outer space. Humans carry microbes and disease with them everywhere and unfortunately, you'll have brought something into the space shuttle.

All of the world's doctors are back on Earth, with their massive selection of treatments and medications. While those onboard your vessel will have medical training, and supplies will have been provided to help you should you become a bit sick, it's just not the same.

Astronauts, therefore, have to take care of their health. They make sure that they monitor their health and keep a good record of all their vitals. It's better to know if someone's sick in advance before the vomit starts floating around the computers. If there are worrying signs or any questions, then the astronauts can ask for medical advice from Earth. Hopefully, it won't be anything too serious.

With a trip to Mars, you'll be taking the longest trip in space ever, so there'll be some interesting discoveries about how space affects the human body. Look after yourself and write it all down.

7. Visiting the best restaurant in the galaxy

If you take a left just before you get to *Markarian 231* and continue straight until you reach *JADES-GS-z13-O,* then you'll find a fantastic burger restaurant that's just perfect after a long trip. Unfortunately, those destinations are impossible to get to, so you'll have to settle for second best while you're in space.

While propelling toward Mars, your vessel will be the best restaurant in the galaxy (not on Earth). All astronauts are provided with enough food (and maybe a little bit more than that) to last for the duration of their mission, and it's vitally important you eat properly. Humans require a lot of vitamins and the right nutrition to keep themselves healthy. It's also worth noting that eating is going to be one of the activities to *do* every day, so astronauts come to enjoy mealtimes.

The food isn't always the most pleasant, however. Fresh ingredients won't last long in space, and there's no way of fitting a full kitchen onboard a spacecraft; it's not a good use of weight. Most spacecraft will come fitted with some things to help prepare food such as an oven, a kettle, or microwave, but you won't be preparing a full roast chicken any time soon.

Food and drinks are all prepared long in advance to last the time required. In your case, that may very well be a year and a half. Some food might be dehydrated or in powdered form, but it'll keep you satiated and healthy.

8. If it ain't broke...look again, it might be broken

Luckily for you and the astronauts that are engineers, there'll be a never-ending stream of 'fixing things' tasks to keep you busy. Equipment will regularly need servicing, cleaning, or mending, and items like air filters or computer systems will need to be checked to ensure they're working properly.

This is vital to ensuring that all is well on the ship, but it will become a bit of a chore. You'll be given supplies and tools to help maintain the vessel, but that doesn't make it any less irritating. The astronauts who trained as engineers typically find themselves having to work on this constantly.

Though it's boring, be diligent in checking everything. You'll want to know early if there's a serious problem with the shuttle's computers.

9. Observations

Observing is just a fancy word for 'looking,' and it's something that we do all the time. You might 'observe' a dog pee all over the floor of your kitchen. Sometimes we 'observe' our friend getting told off by a teacher because it's very funny. When we observe, we learn something and watch as something happens.

This 'observing' will go together with the science experiments. It's all about collecting information so that others may learn as much as they can from your mission. Observations of planets, areas of the galaxy, and the behavior of your colleagues are all carried out and recorded very carefully.

This might seem a bit silly or, even worse, boring - but it's actually very worthwhile work. You may be observing Earth, as you speed toward Mars, and notice something small happen that we haven't noticed before. You might observe the sun exhibiting weird behavior. Hopefully, you won't observe a comet smash into the planet you've just left, but even still, that would be good to know too.

Make sure your glasses are clean! You've got observations to carry out.

10. Relax

Chill, zonk out, let your hair down, calm down, be Zen, take a chill pill, chillax, and take it easy.

There is time to relax on your space shuttle. If you work every hour of the day, before having six terrible hours of sleep then you're going to be constantly tired, irritable, and bad at your job.

Astronauts will make sure they get a chance to relax each day. Just like on Earth, this time is vital for your happiness and well-being. When humans stop working, relax, and make space to think, they become happier. What better place is there to stop and think than thousands of miles from the stress of human life on Earth, gazing at the stars?

Many astronauts report finding amazing peace while on their missions, not working. Perhaps you'll find time to think and come up with a great title for the book you'll write when you get back home.

WHY MARS?

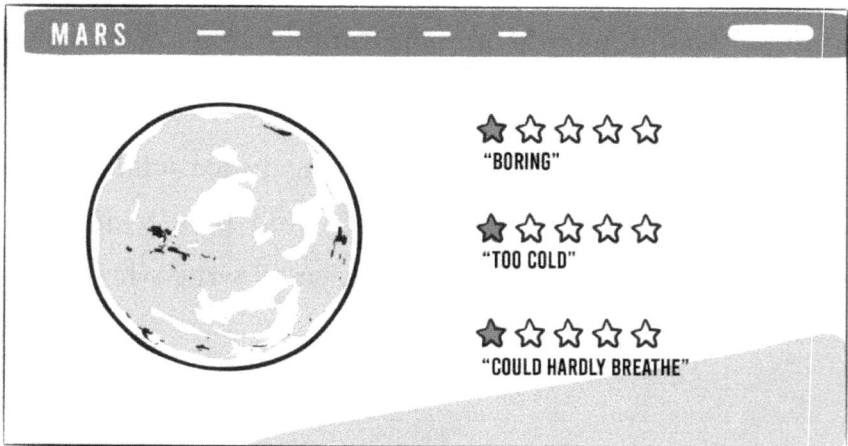

Somewhere on your journey, traveling at a velocity that no human has ever experienced before, a question pops into your mind:

"Why are we going to Mars?"

You hadn't thought about it before - it just seemed obvious that going to Mars was the thing to do - but why?! This chapter is all about that.

You're going to learn about the planet, what makes it special, and why we're so obsessed with our closest planetary neighbor. Hopefully, by the end of this chapter, you'll understand why Mars has occupied the minds of astronauts, scientists, sci-fi writers, nerds, and stargazers for centuries.

1. A few facts about Mars

Before we get started on the whole 'why' of it all, here's a brief introduction to the planet Mars.

Mars is the fourth planet from the Sun, neighboring Earth, which is the third planet. It's about half the size of Earth and is often referred to as the 'Red Planet' due to its reddish appearance. This is caused by a buildup of iron oxide, or rust, on its surface.

Mars can be home to gigantic dust storms that last for months at a time, and the planet exists at a cool -193°F. The planet's air is not suitable for humans. It's made of carbon dioxide, so we'd all choke to death if we tried to breathe there (before we froze to death!).

Mars' atmosphere is also very thin, far thinner than on Earth. This means that harmful radiation gets through, making human existence even more difficult on the red planet. You won't be alone there; you might find the Mars Rovers mentioned in Chapter Two if you look hard enough!

We already told you that Mars is home to the tallest volcano in the Solar System, *Olympus Mons*, but it also has one of the biggest canyons in the Solar System, called the *Valles Marineris*, which is 2,500 miles long. Go and see them both if you have time.

Excited? Good!

2. More science!

You should have seen this coming. Why do we want to go to Mars? For science!

Mars has been observed in greater detail than any other planet beyond Earth, but there's so much more to discover by having a real astronaut on the surface. The experiments that you and your team carry out will provide amazing results that are otherwise impossible to gather.

When you're there, you'll be able to discover more about Mars' history. You might accurately map the different areas of the planet, and you'll be able to report on its climate and weather. You could even name bits of it after yourself:

"I claim this mountain in my name! It is now to be called Alice Mountain!"

3. Plan B

Sometimes things go wrong, just ask the dinosaurs. Some 65 million years ago, the Earth looked very different, and gigantic, terrifying monsters stomped around being the undisputed rulers of our planet. Then, along came a massive meteor that smashed into the planet and killed 90% of all life.

Sometimes, just sometimes, things do go wrong.

People like to theorize about the 'end of the world,' or what might cause serious damage to the planet we live on. Currently, human activity is causing harm to the Earth, and we're seeing the effects of climate change. However, we could have another meteor visit or something completely random that means we need to leave the Earth we're on.

So, where could we go? Well, Mars! Mars is seen as a potential 'plan B' to Earth, should things go pear-shaped here. Part of your job is to set up the first human activity there so that we might continue existing in case of tragedy here on Earth.

No pressure.

4. For fun?

Reaching Mars will be the most incredible achievement for human technology. To think that we started thousands of years ago, emerged from the caves, then worked out how to make a wheel, and before we knew it, we were launching into Mars. Well, is that not a reason enough to go, then what is?

Humans want to go to Mars partly to test themselves and prove that they can do it. This mission will challenge human beings in a way that has never been done before. The test on your mind, as well as the test on the best technology ever created, will be an amazing chance to prove that we can succeed when the odds are stacked against us!

You'll inspire millions of children; they'll watch you and marvel at what's possible. The next generation of incredible scientists, businesspeople, astronauts, doctors, teachers, builders, architects, and all sorts may be inspired because of you going to Mars. Isn't that worth it?

5. The first step

When you reach Mars, you'll establish some human presence on another planet for the first time. This could represent the first step of many.

During your trip, you'll likely set up a small station that you can live in, conduct experiments on the planet, assess what can be done there, and leave. But the next journey might push it a bit further, and the next one further still. After a couple of decades, we might even have a city on Mars. Humanopolis!

From there, the possibilities really are endless. Rockets could be launched from Mars to other planets, starting this whole process again across the entire Solar System. After a few centuries, perhaps we'll be exploring other galaxies in the Milky Way and becoming an intergalactic power, felt across the Universe.

That could all start with you going to Mars…, surely, they'd make a statue of you, or at least name a city after you.

6. Man United

Throughout this book, you may have noticed that humans tend to work together when it comes to space. Here on Earth, there are many problems and wars between countries. We fight over resources and have numerous disagreements, and that doesn't do much to make the world a better place.

However, in space, it's all new to us. No country can accomplish the task of exploring space on its own; all of humanity must work together to succeed. The fact that you even get to Mars will only be possible if all space organizations across the globe work together to get you there.

That's another reason to take this mission on. It would be nice if it led to better friendships between countries on Earth. That alone might be worth all the billions of dollars and effort it will take to get you there.

7. Searching for life

Do you believe that there is alien life *out there* somewhere? Many people do - in fact, 65% of Americans believe so.

Given that the Universe appears to be infinite, stretching out forever, it seems unlikely that there isn't something else out there living. What are the chances that the only living creatures in the whole Universe are situated here, on Earth?

Most NASA scientists are confident that we may one day meet aliens, but we'll need to work pretty hard to find them. This brings us back to Mars.

NASA scientists have discovered that water has been on Mars in the past, and four billion years ago, conditions were right for animals to live on the planet. We now think that there may be evidence of lakes, rivers, and deep oceans on Mars.

On Earth, life needs water to exist, so perhaps the same is true on Mars. When you go there, you'll be able to investigate whether water is still on the planet in some form and whether life may have been there at some time. Who knows, perhaps something's still hiding out there…

8. Halting climate change

Mars is billions of years old, likely as old as Earth. Throughout the years of spinning around the Sun, it's had some changes. We've already learned that water has been and gone, and we're also sure that the climate there will have gone through some serious changes.

When you're up there on the Red Planet, NASA is hoping that you'll figure out exactly what has changed there and why. If you can work out what happened on Mars, then we might be able to use that information to fight climate change here on Earth.

Climate change is causing serious problems for humans on Earth, so any answers you come back with will be highly valuable.

9. Roll yer sleeves up!

Did you know that being a farmer is one of the most important jobs on the planet? Not the politicians, or the musicians, or the police officers!

Farmers are crucial to humans because they grow 99% of our food. It doesn't matter if you eat animals, are vegetarian, or are vegan, farmers across the world grow the food you put into your mouth, and you should be very grateful. Because of advanced farming techniques, a banana can be grown in South America before being eaten in West Japan only a few weeks later. It's amazing really.

So, while you're up there on Mars, miles away from any fresh food, it will be worth your while to see if you can grow something there. It's all well and good considering putting people on Mars, but they can't stay there if they can't make food. It'll take some problem-solving, but if a single carrot can be grown on Mars, then it's a wonderful sign that we might just be able to live there after all.

10.   The true wealth is our health

This multi-billion (perhaps trillion) dollar mission to explore where we've never been before might just offer up some answers regarding our health.

Firstly, you might discover a mineral or some microscopic bacteria that help doctors fight diseases here on Earth. This might save people from illnesses such as cancer or Alzheimer's. Admittedly, this is only if you're very lucky and know what to look for. But still, that's a nice thing to consider.

Secondly, the journey to Mars will be the longest amount of time any person has ever spent traveling in outer space. This places your crew in a unique position to test out medical equipment while in weightlessness. Medical companies will be desperately trying to encourage your crew to use *their* equipment to fight medical problems out in space. Any medical progress out there in space could mean huge amounts of medical progress back here on Earth.

Basically, this trip could do a lot for our health. Not *your* health. It'll probably make you ill and miserable on the ship. But don't think about that—think about the millions and millions of lives your research up there could save!

CAN WE LIVE ON MARS?

Unfortunately, the title of this chapter can be answered in three words:

"No…, not yet."

In present-day times, humans are not going to be able to move to Mars; it's simply not possible. Sorry to be the bearer of bad news.

However, all is not pointless and lost. Though we aren't about to be given our new address of *75 Mars Way* any time soon, several space organizations are drawing up plans for how long-term human habitation of Mars might work. This chapter is all about that: How do we move on from our mission to moving humans onto our new home?

Interestingly, the humans on Mars will be known as Martians, so I guess we can think of them as the first confirmed aliens!

1. Housing

Firstly, we need to consider *where* people will live on Mars. There's no shortage of room, of course, but we need to make houses that keep people safe and happy in their strange new homes.

As we know, Mars is incredibly cold and its atmosphere is lower than Earth's, as well as unbreathable by humans. This means that the housing has to be able to keep out the cold and not accidentally let loads of Martian air in.

What seems likely is that homes for people on Mars might have to be underground, so that the rock and surface material provides some extra protection from radiation and the cold. This might make people a little bit miserable, however, so we'd have to have some larger inflatable structures on the surface of the planet.

The houses underground will have to be supplied with constant heating and air supply. If this fails, then everyone on Mars will simply die. So, housing is quite important! Other than this, we may have to construct a fake Sun that provides the inhabitants of Mars with fake sunlight.

Does it sound good so far? Or is it sounding like the worst holiday of all time?

2. Life support

This was mentioned in the housing section, but it's worth thinking about for longer. A 'life support system' is going to be 100% crucial to the success of human life on Mars. These systems are machines that would help keep humans living by providing key functions.

These systems would have to recycle everything that is used on Mars. This means that the air, water, and human waste would have to be filtered, cleaned, and recycled to all be consumed again. Yes, you heard that right. Human urine and poo will have to be re-used while people are on Mars.

That might sound extreme, but you know by now that it takes months to get to Mars. The Martians can't spend their lives waiting for supplies from Earth, so they'll have to get the most out of what they already have up there.

The life support systems will ensure that the Martians stay alive and will need expert engineers to keep them working. Can you imagine living underground, eating recycled human waste, and breathing in air that's been breathed in over 1,000 times before?

Okay, don't put that on the leaflets.

3. Everyone's an astronaut!

Whenever we send a human away from their home planet, we need to make sure they're expertly prepared for *anything*. This means that everyone will get astronaut training to prepare them for emergencies and to adapt to the strange challenges of Mars.

This is going to cost a *lot* of money and will slow things down. But we can't have our very first Martians being useless at everything; they need to be able to help if everything goes wrong when they're on Mars.

This, upsettingly, will also mean that you won't be special as an astronaut anymore. Everyone's going to be one.

4. Menu du Jour

It's dinner time! Or rather, you *hope* it's going to be dinner time.

As far as we can tell, Mars has nothing edible on it and no water. It's not exactly the hottest spot in the galaxy for a gourmet meal. So, how are the Martians going to get decent food in their new home?

The first step will take place before the big move to Mars. Earth scientists will attempt to genetically modify vegetables and fruit, so they can survive in enriched Martian soil, in the Martian atmosphere. If this is accomplished, then Martians will spend many years farming to build up their store of food and create functioning farms. They'll figure out which vegetables are best grown at what time of the year, which flourish, and which need a bit more help in greenhouses to grow.

The next step is to figure out how to make Coca-Cola on Mars.

Only joking - it's to figure out how to keep up water levels.

Mars has large deposits of ice as we do on our North and South poles. This ice could be melted to provide water for the Martians, and we've already mentioned the whole 'drinking human urine' thing too. As well as this, machines could work on making water out of tiny molecules. It wouldn't be a natural way of producing water, but it might be the best way to keep up water levels.

You'll have to be vegetarian on Mars. Cows are not about to make the seven-month journey to Mars, only to be turned into a thousand burgers when it lands.

5. Will *The Simpsons* be on Mars?

By this point, we've dealt with the most significant elements of survival. The Martians are setting up sustainable food and water while creating their homes underneath the surface of the planet where it's hotter. They're doing well, but they can't keep this up without *energy*.

Luckily Mars receives tons of energy every day. It's all free and is available for the Martians to use without having to work too hard. Can you work out where from?

That's right, from the Sun!

We have invented solar power here on Earth, large solar panels that absorb sunlight and easily convert it into usable energy. Mars gets plenty of sunlight and so has plenty of energy available. This means that the life support systems can keep running, the water robots keep making water, and Martians can watch television (perhaps).

6. Explorers

The age of exploration on Earth is over. For hundreds and thousands of years, human beings have sailed, flown, and walked around Earth discovering almost every part of it. The only bit of the planet that isn't fully mapped out is the ocean. For an obvious reason, we can't all go down there to discover it.

However, the Martians are now tasked with discovering a whole new world. Their task will be traveling away from their homes to find every nook and cranny that Mars has to offer.

Before too long, new regions will be named after the Martians that discovered them, written onto maps. The exploration is going to be crucial to the survival of the Martians. With enough digging, they may find resources to help society flourish, and to study whether the planet may be able to hold life outside of their underground homes.

What will you name the colossal mountain that you discover? (Mounty McMountainface, obviously).

7. Best ways of getting around

You've already read about the rovers that got to Mars a long time before you. It turns out that they're fantastic at driving across the rocky landscape of the Red Planet, so Martians will probably be building and using similar vehicles for a long time to come.

Rovers will make the mission of exploration easy. The specially designed machines will enable quick navigation of vast canyons, heaven-scraping mountains, and gaping caverns. Over time, it's thought that a railway could be invented to provide easy public transport for the Martians as the settlement grows.

With more exploration and more transport, new towns may be founded. The towns may grow into colossal cities with vibrant communities, connected by trains and electric rover-buses.

It's all starting to come together, isn't it?

8. A Mars Bar a day keeps the doctor well away

In all this positivity and endless possibilities that could only be a few decades away from reality, there is a scary threat. Humans are supposed to be on planet Earth. Humans have spent thousands of years getting used to the various diseases on our planet. Our bodies are specially designed to fight off Earth's illnesses, and they do so remarkably well.

However, this won't be the case on Mars. If Mars has bacteria, then it has diseases. If it has diseases, then they'll be wholly different from Earthborn illnesses. So, the Martians are going to get sick.

Some doctors will certainly journey to Mars. They'll be provided with high-tech medical equipment and supplies that will cope with many different emergencies. Likely, these Martians will also communicate with Earth doctors who can give more advice about how to treat sicknesses and maladies.

The first few generations of Martians are going to encounter some new diseases and will need to be alert to stop them from becoming too deadly.

9. Support and communication

Do you remember when you were traveling to Mars, on that first trip? The first astronaut to ever make that incredible journey into the great unknown? We spoke about the fact that it was going to be tough for you to cope with. Well, it turns out that doesn't get better for Martians either.

We've said it repeatedly: Humans are from Earth. It doesn't matter how great we try to make the settlement on Mars, the Martians are still going to struggle emotionally. In their underground homes, onboard the trains, and working for their survival on farms, they're going to miss Earth.

The isolation from the rest of humanity may make the Martians sad as they tirelessly work on their task. For those of us back on Earth, we will make sure to contact the Martians regularly. Humanity will devise a strong internet-like technology that can travel across space, connecting all people across our two planets.

Doing so will be key to the success of any such Martian settlement.

10. Entertainment

Leading on from the previous point, we can also help the Martians be happy by providing them with some entertainment.

But what does Martian entertainment look like? They won't quite have the level of freedom that we have on Earth, of course. They'll have to be properly suited up when outside; otherwise, all entertainment will be indoors.

Hiking and walking around Mars will be available to the Martians, as long as they're in their space suits. They'll also have the ability to exercise in indoor gyms, as well as access digital entertainment like video games, watching movies, and reading. By the time Martians are on Mars, they'll likely be provided with Virtual Reality experiences. Virtual Reality will allow a chance to escape - or to pretend to, anyway.

Other than this, they can carry out many hobbies that we have on Earth such as photography, art, and writing.

All in all, they'll have some entertainment. If the internet's good enough, they may very well be able to stream the latest Marvel movie and watch it before it even gets to Disney+.

ARE WE ALL ALONE OUT HERE?

By this point, we've covered most aspects of your travel to Mars. The whole time that you're engaged in this important mission, everyone on Earth will have been wondering if you're going to become the first person to ever meet a real-life alien.

Now, you very well may not. The Mars Rovers haven't seen an alien on the planet yet, but that doesn't mean that you won't. This chapter is going to prepare you for the eventuality that you meet an alien.

There's no *Guide to Meeting Aliens* book out there, but this carefully researched chapter will bring you what information we humans have gathered about beings from another world.

1. What does NASA think?

Earlier in this book we gave you the statistic that 65% of Americans believe that aliens exist. It's all very well and good mentioning that statistic, but what do the qualified nerds and experts at NASA think?

NASA says that one of its key goals "is the search for life in the Universe." Most NASA scientists are confident that there is life *out there*, and NASA has made attempts to make contact with little green men from all over the Universe.

Do you remember the Voyager spacecraft from the second chapter? The spacecraft that are on a one-way trip, now entering deep space, impossibly far from Earth where they were made?

Well, onboard each of the Voyager crafts is something called a Golden Record. It's a vinyl record (like old people play their music on) that contains several pieces of information.

NASA scientists decided to put these records on the Voyager crafts so that if an alien finds them, they can find out what humans are and what is valuable to them. The record gives an idea of what, in 1977, was seen as a 'key understanding' of human life. Here are a few things included:

- Images (116) including of the Solar System, human bodies, areas of interest on Earth, chimpanzees, the Taj Mahal, a museum, a dog, an astronaut, and some sheet music for *cavatina*.
- Sounds (several) of Earth such as a barking dog, a chimpanzee, wind, footsteps, laughter, a heartbeat, a tractor, a train, and a kiss.
- Audi tracks (55) of people saying hello in different languages.
- A selection of music includes traditional indigenous Australian, European classical, and 'Jonny B. Goode' by Chuck Berry.

If an alien finds the record, then they *might* be able to extract some of the information here. But they'll have to be pretty clever aliens! If they can get the information from the record, though, they'll probably think we're incredibly old-fashioned for using vinyl records.

2. Aliens are nothing new

When you think of aliens, you may think of a futuristic civilization that possesses impossible technology. Most people assume that the idea of aliens is a modern phenomenon because of how often they are featured in our modern movies and television shows.

In reality, however, the idea of aliens is not new at all. Some of the most famous ancient civilizations, from thousands of years ago, had myths and stories about aliens. Hindu mythology mentions 'Vimanas,' a flying craft (like a UFO) that was piloted by alien beings. The Ancient Egyptians wrote and painted stories of encounters with beings from other stars or planets. Native American legends also talk of 'star people.' The star people would descend from the heavens to provide humans with knowledge and wisdom.

For thousands, even tens of thousands, of years, humans have thought that alien beings were present *out there*. While our ancient ancestors would have had difficulty imagining the technology needed to travel to other planets, it's interesting to know that the basic concept of aliens has remained a constant in human culture.

3. Have we already been visited?

Cast your mind back to 1947. Okay, you probably weren't born in 1947, but just think about it. There are no mobile phones and no televisions, and people are recovering from World War II, looking forward to a positive future.

In June, America became a bit obsessed with the idea of flying saucers, and the idea of a saucer has stayed in our culture ever since. Private pilot Kenneth Arnold reported that he'd seen nine flying saucers in the sky near Mount Rainier, Washington; the newspapers printed his story repeatedly. Suddenly everyone was looking skyward, sure that they'd see evidence of little aliens in large ships, coming to abduct us all.

The craze of the flying saucer came to a head in July, with what is known as the "Roswell Incident." A local ranch owner in Roswell, New Mexico noticed some strange parts of a machine on his ranch. He was alerted by the recent 'flying saucer craze' and became convinced it was a UFO (Unidentified Flying Object).

He reported the find to the local sheriff, and the authorities were called in. He was told that the debris belonged to a weather balloon and was nothing to worry about. It wasn't until the 1970s that an Army officer who dealt with the Roswell incident admitted that it may have been a lie. Officer Marcel says that the 'weather balloon' story is a cover-up, and it may have been a UFO all along.

We have no confirmation of Earth being visited by aliens yet, and the old stories have been explained away as hoaxes. But who knows, perhaps the middle of the saucer craze was the perfect time to sneak in for a look...

4. The Drake Equation

We explained before that the Universe is really, really big. Well, that's still true. Current scientific estimates say that the Universe is getting bigger all the time and that it's virtually impossible to know where we sit within it. Mind-blowing stuff, but it leaves us with a question about aliens.

How many might there be out there?

Well, we have an answer. Supposedly there are approximately 15,600,000 different alien civilizations in the Universe.

This number is conjured up using a very clever sum, created by Dr. Frank Drake, a very clever scientist. The number comes from looking at data based on our Solar System. It's all very approximate and was never really meant to be taken as an exact guess of the number of aliens. But it's fun to think that our super-smart scientists can figure out that there could be more than 15 million different civilizations out there.

Earthlings are just one civilization. By the way, the term "Earthlings" includes humans, monkeys, elephants, whales, squid, spiders, zebras, giraffes, and all living things on this planet. Just think about another 15 million full worlds of creatures. That's a lot to explore.

5. The Fermi Paradox

"Okay then, clever clogs Dr. Frank Drake, if there are so many millions of billions of trillions of aliens out there, why haven't we met one yet?"

This is the question you may ask, and it would be a good one. This is where the Fermi Paradox comes in.

A paradox is something that is true but sounds like it shouldn't be. For instance, the sentence "This sentence is a lie" is a paradox.

If the sentence is lying, then the sentence is true. This means that it isn't a lie, which it says it is.

If the sentence is telling the truth, then the sentence is telling us that it is a lie.

The Fermi Paradox says that it's very strange that we have no evidence for the existence of any aliens, but our clever scientists all agree that there are probably lots of them out there. We even have a formula that guesses that there are millions of them!

This means that we must wonder, "Why haven't we met any aliens yet?"

There are a few answers to this paradox.

Firstly, the Universe is huge, and though there are probably millions of civilizations, they could be such a long distance away that they haven't traveled anywhere near us. Secondly, it might be that there are very few civilizations out there, and perhaps they can't travel to another planet. If we visit them, we may see a planet of animals without intelligent abilities.

For whatever reason, it's just not happened yet, and the Fermi Paradox makes us think about why it is that it hasn't happened. Perhaps an intelligent race of aliens has seen us and is planning how they should first say hello?

6. Wow! Signal

On August 15, 1977, Ohio State University picked up a strong radio signal on their Big Ear radio telescope. The radio telescope was used to search for alien life, and this made everyone involved in the program very excited.

The signal lasted 72 seconds and didn't have a detectable sound, but it was there. When it was detected, an astronomer wrote the word "Wow!" down, to signify how surprised he was. The signal is now known as the 'Wow! Signal' as a result.

What makes this strange is that the signal hasn't been observed since, despite searching for it. It could have been anything, but it so far remains the strongest possible evidence for alien life.

7. Our first visitor

As you know, Earth is the only planet inhabited by anything in the Solar System. As no one seems to have yet realized we're here, we don't tend to get too many visitors. That is until 2017 when the first visit from outside of our star system was confirmed.

The Haleakalā Observatory in Hawaii spotted an object in October 2017. The object was between 300 and 3,000 feet long, and between 115 and 548 feet wide. It was traveling at a top speed of 54,059 miles per second, which was far too fast for an object from the Solar System.

This had to have come from another star system.

It was named 'Oumuamua,' which means "a messenger from afar arriving first" and is our first confirmed sighting of something from another star system in our area! The object could have been anything and was unlikely to have been a contact by aliens. But it does mean that things *could* travel here and arrive in one piece. What will be next?

8. Is it all just a load of...crop?

An image associated with aliens here on Earth is the 'crop circle.' Ever since the flying saucer craze, crop circles have been turning up in farmers' fields.

Crop circles are usually found in a field of wheat or corn. Farmers go out in the morning to see a perfect circle or series of circles, squashed into the crops. For a while, this had people convinced that this was evidence of flying saucers landing on Earth. They certainly had farmers spooked for a while during the 1950s.

Unfortunately, it's very easy to do this as a human being, and almost all of the crop circles have been proven to have been made by unruly teenagers or bored adults.

We will need more conclusive evidence than a squashed bit of corn!

9. SETI and what to do with first contact

In 1972, an organization was created comprising scientists and researchers. The organization was called the Search for Extraterrestrial Intelligence (SETI) program, and it is solely dedicated to trying to prove that aliens exist.

The program hasn't yet found anything, but by Jove, they are trying!

SETI has helpfully decided what 'first contact' will probably look like if it happens. Firstly, they're sure that it'll be a radio signal, not an actual visit. Aliens probably won't just fly by to say hello; they'll test the water by contacting us remotely. If they do this, then the message they send will have been at least 100 years old. So, it may take 100 years for a simple 'hello' to reach us from when they send it.

SETI has said that responding is the tricky part. If aliens send a radio transmission, then theoretically anyone on Earth who has the right equipment could hear it and respond. So, an alien may send a 'hello' and get four million "Hi's," "How ya doings," and one million descriptions of what a dog is.

So, our initial contact may be a bit cluttered. If we can have more control then SETI recommends sending a picture of a rock, or something as simple as a rock, so that aliens can understand us.

Either way, our first conversation will take hundreds of years to have. It's not quite as exciting as *E.T.*, but it's something.

10.   Is there an Earth 2?

Humanity hasn't been the kindest to our Earth. Over the last 300 years, we've increased our use of resources and begun polluting on a large scale, which has left the planet in a 'not-so-great' state. We're working on halting climate change caused by this, but it's going to require some work.

So, what if there was a second Earth, nearby, that we could all just hop on and forget about Earth 1?

Well, good news! We have several.

Over the years, NASA has discovered many planets that seem to be 'Earth-like'. This means a planet with an atmosphere like ours, that could have water on it, and that is about as far from their star as Earth is from the Sun. While these are exciting discoveries, they are all impossibly far away. We currently don't have the ability to get anywhere close to the planets, so we're not about to visit them any time soon. We'll just have to try Mars first. In the meantime, here's some information about the Earth-like planets we've found so far:

- *Proxima Centauri b* was discovered in 2016. The planet is a little bit bigger than Earth and is at the perfect distance from its star. It's also in the nearest Solar System to ours! This means that with our current technology, it would only take us 19,000 years to get to.
- *The TRAPPIST-1 System* is a star system that has several habitable planets within it, giving us lots of choices. The planets seem quite Earth-like in size and should be habitable. These are further away than "Proxima Centauri b," however, and would take us 178,184 years to travel to.
- *Kepler-452b,* otherwise known as "Earth's cousin" has many similarities to our planet. It's a lot bigger but is in

ideal proximity to its star; it may be perfect for humans to go and live on. The big problem is that this one will take us 6,299,454 years to get to.

You can see the problem. Getting to the nearest easiest habitable planet is an impossible task right now. The big question for the scientists of the future is whether we can create a spaceship that could get people to any of these planets before its crew dies.

If nothing else, this might help you understand - just a bit - how huge our galaxy and Universe truly are.

FINAL TRANSMISSION

If you read the whole book, then you've taken on a crazy amount of information. You've gazed upon decades of research and risk-taking, all reduced to this brief book. Didn't you do well?

Getting to Mars is no easy task, but it's probably not that far away from happening. The moment a human steps foot on the Red Planet will be the greatest achievement in the history of space exploration. We'll have started our journey into the cosmos, and perhaps you might even be the one to do it. Who knows!

You're likely reading this book because you're interested in space; you might even be *very* interested. Hopefully perusing the pages of this informative guide of space and space travel has only sparked your curiosity further. Every astronaut started as a small child gazing into the night sky, wondering what could be out there, and hoping they'd get to see it for themselves.

Your next task is to keep on learning. This means paying attention in school, watching documentaries, reading books that get more and more complicated as you read them, and becoming a better, smarter person for doing so. Learning is brilliant, and it's at its most brilliantist (not a word, don't use that) when we're learning about something we love. Continue to educate yourself and it won't ever feel like a chore.

Remember to never stop being amazed by space. It's an incredible topic that we barely understand and are doing our best to grasp. Contribute even a little bit to humanity's knowledge and you'll be a hero.

One final fact for you:

If we scaled the Milky Way down to being the same width as the United States of America, the center would be roughly in Kansas and the Solar System would be at about Denver, Colorado. At this scale, with the Milky Way reduced to the size of one of the biggest countries on Earth, our Sun - our star - would be big enough to fit between two ridges of a human's fingerprint.

Look at your own finger now. Find two of your fingerprint ridges, and see just how tiny that is. Then think about how small you are, compared to the whole of the USA.

Remember just how small we are, and that everything might just be possible in this wondrous, expanding Universe of ours.

GLOSSARY

This is a short glossary of spacey terms that you may want to look at. Most of the definitions have been gathered from a list found on NASA's official website of recommended terms that you should know as a space enthusiast.

Refer back to this glossary if you become slightly confused or aren't sure about a word.

Asteroid: Rocks floating around in space. Some are the size of a pick-up truck. Others are hundreds of miles across.

Atmosphere: The gases held by gravity around Earth and other planets.

Atom: The basic, infinitely small, building block of matter. It is made of protons, neutrons, and electrons. There are many different kinds of atoms.

Black hole: A place in space where matter and light cannot escape if they fall in.

Comet: An icy rock that lets off gas and dust, which may form tails when it is flying close to a sun.

Constellation: A group of stars in the sky. They're often named after an animal, object, or person. The stars form certain patterns based on where you are when you look at them.

Cosmos: The Universe is seen as an orderly, harmonious whole.

Dwarf planet: Objects that are round and orbit the Sun, just like planets do. But unlike planets, dwarf planets cannot clear their path around the Sun. A dwarf planet is much smaller than a planet (smaller even than Earth's moon), but it is not a moon. Pluto is the best-known dwarf planets.

Galaxy: A collection of thousands to billions of stars held together by gravity. The galaxy we live in is called the Milky Way.

Gas: A loose collection of atoms moving around each other.

Gravity: A force that pulls matter together.

Greenhouse gas: Gases in the atmosphere that trap heat from the Sun. Some greenhouse gases are carbon dioxide, methane, water vapor, and nitrous oxide.

Light year: It's not a year, or an amount of time at all. It's the distance light travels in one year. It's the same as 5,878,499,810,000 miles. When things are very far away, it's easier to talk about their distance in light years than millions, billions, or trillions of miles.

Mass: The amount of matter something is made of.

Matter: The stuff that everything is made of. Atoms are a tiny bit of matter. Big planets have lots of matter. Even you are made of matter!

Meteor: The streak of light caused when a meteoroid enters a planet's atmosphere and starts to burn from the heat of friction.

Meteorite: A meteoroid that lands on the surface of a planet.

Meteoroid: A little chunk of rock in space smaller than a pick-up truck. If it were bigger, it would be an asteroid.

Molecule: The smallest unit of a substance that still acts like the main substance. A molecule can be a single atom or a group of atoms. Water is a substance, and one molecule of water is made of two hydrogen atoms and one oxygen atom, which we write as H_2O.

Moon: A natural object that travels around a bigger natural object. Planets can have moons. Dwarf planets can have moons. Even some asteroids have moons! Astronomers usually call them satellites or natural satellites.

NASA: America's space agency. NASA stands for "The National Aeronautics and Space Administration."

Nebula: A cloud of dust or gas found between stars.

Neutron star: A very dense star made mostly of neutrons. It has a very powerful gravitational force nearby because the whole mass of a star is pulled into one object just a few miles across.

Orbit: The curved path that a planet, satellite, or spacecraft moves as it circles around another object.

Particle: A tiny amount or small piece of something.

Planet: A large body in outer space that circles around the Sun or another star.

Probe: An unmanned spacecraft that transmits information about its environment back to Earth.

Radiation: The energy or particles released from sources like radioactive materials, explosions, and chemical reactions.

Radioactive: How we describe some atoms that are unstable. They change into different kinds of atoms and release lots of energy.

Satellite: An object that orbits another object. The moon is actually a satellite. We also say satellite to refer to spacecraft people build that orbit Earth, other planets, moons, asteroids, or other objects out in space.

Solar System: A set that includes a star and all of the matter that orbits it, including planets, moons, asteroids, comets, and other objects.

Spacecraft: A vehicle used for traveling in space.

Speed of Light: Light is the fastest thing in the Universe. It travels 186,282 miles every second.

Star: A ball of shining gas, made mostly of hydrogen and helium, held together by its own gravity. Turning hydrogen into helium creates the energy that makes stars shine.

Sun: The star in the center of our Solar System.

Supernova: The explosion of a star that makes it as bright as a whole galaxy.

Universe: All of space and time, and everything in it. It's everything ever!

Vacuum: An empty space that has no matter.

www.ingramcontent.com/pod-product-compliance
Lightning Source LLC
Chambersburg PA
CBHW060241030426
42335CB00014B/1558